little Mitchie

FINDING FRIENDS AT SCHOOL

MAKING NEW FRIENDS

ANNE ACCARDI

CREATING YOUNG NONFICTION READERS

Little Mitchie books spark curiosity and support early nonfiction reading for students in Grades 2-3. Designed to build vocabulary, support second language learners, and prepare readers for middle-grade content, each book includes helpful tips for parents and educators to build confidence and deepen understanding of the world.

TIPS FOR READING NONFICTION WITH BEGINNING READERS

Talk about Nonfiction

Begin by explaining that nonfiction books give us information that is true. The book will be organized around a specific topic or idea, and we may learn new facts through reading.

Look at the Parts

Most nonfiction books have helpful features. Our *Little Mitchie* titles include color photographs and graphic aids, a table of contents, a glossary, and an index. Share the purpose of these features with your reader.

Color Photos and Graphic Aids

A lot of information can be found by "reading" photos, charts, maps, and other graphic aids found within nonfiction texts. Help your reader learn more about the different ways information can be displayed.

Table of Contents

Located at the front of the book, this list shows the big ideas within the text and the page numbers where they can be found.

Glossary

Located at the back of the book, the glossary defines key words and phrases that are related to the topic. These words and phrases can be found in the text in colored type.

Index

Located at the back of the book, an index is an alphabetical list of topics and the page numbers where they can be found.

With a little help and guidance about reading nonfiction, you can feel good about introducing a young reader to the world of *Little Mitchie* nonfiction books.

Little Mitchie is an imprint of:

Mitchell Lane
PUBLISHERS

2001 SW 31st Avenue
Hallandale, FL 33009
mitchelllanepub.com

First Edition, 2027.

Author: Anne Accardi
Designer: Kathy Walsh
Editor: Kim Thompson

Library of Congress Cataloging-in-Publication Data
Title: Finding Friends at School / by Anne Accardi

Description: Hallandale, FL :
Mitchell Lane Publishers, [2027]

Identifiers:
ISBN 979-8-89260-897-8 (library bound)
ISBN 979-8-90145-054-3 (paperback)
ISBN 979-8-90145-001-7 (eBook)

Library of Congress Control Number: 2026930271

Photo credits: Shutterstock: Cover p1 & 3, arthierry; p 5, WBMUL; p 6, wavebreakmedia; p 8, oneinchpunch; p 9, wavebreakmedia; p 11, SynthEx; p 13, SergeyKlopotov; p 15, Robert Kneschke; p 17, Andril Iemelianenko; p 18, BearFotos; p 21, Monkey Business Images

TABLE OF CONTENTS

Step One

KNOW WHY SCHOOL FRIENDS ARE IMPORTANT

Who do you sit with at lunch? Hang out with at recess? Talk to during class projects? Your school friends!

It is important to have friends at school. They are **kind** to you. They teach you new things. They make you feel like you belong.

FRIENDLY FACT
Quality matters more than **quantity**. Having just one or two good friends makes school more fun.

There are different kinds of friends. Some you know better than others. Some may be in different grades or classes. Some you may see only on the bus. To make new friends, be nice to everyone.

FRIENDLY FACT

A **clique** is a group that does not welcome new friends. They leave others out to make themselves feel popular and cool. This is not what real friendship is about.

Step Two

FACE YOUR FEARS

It can be scary to talk to **peers** you don't know well. You might feel **shy**. You may be afraid of saying the "wrong" thing.

Remind yourself that everyone has feelings like this. People want to be your friend just like you want to be friends with them.

FRIENDLY FACT

Almost half of all kids say they sometimes feel shy. This is okay! Everyone has their own personality and their own **pace**.

Make a plan for meeting new friends. Join a club, team, or other activity. You'll meet kids who share your interests. It is less scary to talk to someone if you have something in common.

CHALLENGE

Make a list of three things you like to do. Find out if there are any groups to join that focus on those activities. They could be at school or in your community.

Step Three

TAKE ACTION!

You are ready to make a new friend! Take a deep breath. Be brave. Start a **conversation**.

Ask someone their name and tell them yours. Share something about yourself. Ask a question that will help you get to know them.

Here are some good conversation starters.

- *My pet was so funny when ______. Do you have a pet?*
- *I think ______ is my favorite sport. What's yours?*
- *Last night I had ______ for dinner. What's your favorite dinner?*
- *I want to ______ when I grow up. How about you?*
- *At recess, I like to ______. Do you want to play?*

Use **body language** to show you are friendly and **open**. Look at your new friend. Smile and nod. When you see them, wave hello.

CHALLENGE

Practice friendly body language in the mirror. After you've practiced, ask a family member to give you tips.

Keep talking to your new friend. Focus on things you have in common. Chat about favorite movies, foods, or games.

Invite your new friend to play. You can even spend time together outside of school. Ask your family to set up a playdate.

"You can't stay in your corner of the forest waiting for others to come to you. You have to go to them sometimes."

—A. A. Milne, Winnie-the-Pooh

Step Four

KEEP GOING

Once you've made a new friend at school, you can make even more friends through them. Start conversations with their friends. Invite more people to join your group.

School is a great place to make friends. Don't be afraid to take the first step!

Top Tips

Join clubs or activities.

Use friendly body language.

Introduce yourself.

Ask questions.

Set up playdates.

GLOSSARY

body language (BAH-dee LANG-gwij) the thoughts and feelings your face and body communicate without using words

clique (klik) a small group of friends who do not easily allow others to join them

conversation (kahn-vur-SAY-shuhn) a talk between two or more people

kind (kinde) nice; caring; friendly

open (OH-puhn) willing to do new things, meet new people, or listen to new ideas

pace (pase) speed

peers (peerz) people who are the same age as you or in the same situation as you

quantity (KWAHN-ti-tee) number; amount

shy (shye) uncomfortable around people you don't know well

FURTHER READING

Bailey, Jenn. *A Friend for Henry*. Chronicle Books, 2019.

Sperring, Mark. *When You Meet My Friend*. Tiger Tales, 2026.

Stein, Joshua. *Make New Friends*. Abrams Books for Young Readers, 2025.

ON THE INTERNET

Greater Good in Action: 36 Questions to Help Kids Make Friends
ggia.berkeley.edu/practice/36_questions_to_help_kids_make_friends
Find conversation starters for meeting new people.

National Geographic Kids: How to Be an Awesome Friend
kids.nationalgeographic.com/pages/article/friend
Learn tips for making and keeping friends.

INDEX